THAT BROKE INTO SHINING CRYS

by the same author

SOHO

RICHARD SCOTT

That Broke into Shining Crystals

faber

First published in 2025
by Faber & Faber Ltd
The Bindery, 51 Hatton Garden
London EC1N 8HN

Typeset by Hamish Ironside
Printed in the UK by Martins the Printers

A CIP record for this book is available from the British Library

ISBN 978–0–571–39131–8

Printed and bound in the UK on FSC® certified paper in line with our continuing
commitment to ethical business practices, sustainability and the environment.
For further information see faber.co.uk/environmental-policy

10 9 8 7 6 5 4 3 2 1

And grateful that a thing
So terrible – had been endured –
I told my Soul to sing –
EMILY DICKINSON

The archive in the mouth and the archive is on fire
PETER GIZZI

Contents

I STILL LIFES

It is a matter of intensity, of will. It is possible to look at a painting and not see anything at all. There must be an offering of the self before the painting will open. There must be an intensity, or the past will stay locked.

RACHEL CUSK

Who are these coming to the sacrifice?
JOHN KEATS

Still Life with Rose

Like a foreskin being pulled back, the damask
reveals – pelvic bowl of pink-fringed shadow,
dense sweet-meat bloom, coral'd cave, puce
empyrean with no vanishing point, planetary blush!
So let me in – where everything is new-born
and crystalline, paused and protected – into that other
world, that high-shine place of safety, arranged
and sparking up like a bower. Almost every day,
for some moments, I think about him – the black
stems, thorns that can prick so deeply, whorl
of serrated leaves, all just beneath, around – still
gorgeousness – your petal'd cumulus, your constancy –
helps me live. O rose keep on stunning for me –
for all us boys who have been ruined by men.

Still Life with Lobster, Fruit and Timepiece

I have wanted to be the lobster:
all that muscle, that
rose-orange exoskeleton,

terracotta warrior toy, ruddy
crusher claw, the
blackest eye shining. So

scrappy. So robust. So very
protected but
even he ended up on the

table – broken apart, belly
opened – men,
silver, flashing above him.

Even he was left emptied,
scooped out, a
pile of bits – unreassemblable.

And the tangerine is falling out
of its peel. And
the melon's seeded grimace.

I don't need to see the pocket-
watch, its frayed
carnelian ribbon unspooled

like an entrail, to know all
time here has
stopped. And that one black eye

staring out beyond the canvas.
And all the
people who just watched.

Still Life with Lemons in a Wicker Basket

I don't want a basket full of lemons –
I've had enough bitter times.
Give me instead the flame-licked day-
lilies opening so hard they are

breaking their own backs or that
little porcelain bowl – its blue
arcadia scrawled delicately as scar
tissue – or a sip of that make-

believe tea steaming away for a
century or two, or that woven basket –
such regimented beauty – wicker
sticks lined up all in a row like a little

boy's ribs. Yes, give me instead those
two carnations – prismatic bbs –
so very white like how quartz is some-
times white and kind of blinding –

true opposite of all these shadows
I have been carrying around in me
for the longest time – shadows
that are his hands moving across the light,

that are his hands moving across my
body. O the hypersensitivity of the victim
who finds even these lemons –
their muscular rinds rendered in such

forensic light – threatening. Who is
crying now because sometimes he misses
being looked at. Who is older now.
Who goes into galleries and clocks

the still lifes and feels this seismic
mirroring as he encounters their
codification – for if he cannot unpick him-
self, he can at least unpick the

lemons, lilies, basket and bowl. Bright
symbols waiting for the sore and
broken mind to rush in, inhabit. Brilliant
alarms burning against complacency.

Still Life with Basket of Songbirds

Flax and peach-crowned hoopoe
slumped next to this scarlet finch
with a human expression. Or
the sandpiper – the unlikely pin-
slender flute of his beak, stilled.
Or this bluethroat – silent, sfumato
and curled embryonically against
the blackcap and sulphur-hued
serin, or canary. The curator writes,
alludes to the noble pursuit of
falconry. And yes, to the left
of the basket looms the stiff-backed
hawk, talon-deep in songbird
and absolutely triggering. The hunt
is already over. Little lifetimes
spent in the falcon's onyx glare.
Song on the cusp of ingestion.
Audible only in the prismatic glints –
hematite, orpiment, gallstone –
colouring the austere and feathered
darkness of 1612. The curator writes,
sometimes Peeters painted her
reflection in goblets and gilt cups.
How the self intrudes. Reorders.
Ruins. Are you the thrush, Clara?
Or am I? Shut-beaked, gone limp
in the basket, unbearable patination
of delicate spots. Little upside-
down hearts speckling our breast.
And my heart hurts, now. Aches.
Is talon-pierced and torn open.

Still Life with Three Roses

The three stages of this rose –
bud, bloom, overblown –
are like the three stages of
this boy – pre-trauma, mol-
estation, PTSD – only
none of this was petal'd or
remotely like these extraordinary
shades sliding from blush to
rhodonite to empyrean – only
perhaps this being seen – the
pearlescent beetle alights
on the filament – was
unexpectedly beautiful – drop
of photorealistic dew
on the stem – maybe these roses
are like the stages of
grooming – friendship and then
I can't quite remember
exactly what came next – corolla
edge ringed in a deeper and
bleeding colour – quite how
he made it all happen – delicate
sepal, pistil – also I know
I am not supposed to tell
anyone – craquelure rosehips
scattered about the base
of the urn – so don't tell anyone,
Richard – a darkness –
pink, rotate, gaping – that
makes the petals of my
mouth wind shut when
they should be screaming –

Still Life with Snail, Oyster, Spoon and Shallot Vinegar

O I should have been the
snail. Living phallus that can
hide when threatened. But
I'm the oyster. Quivery ashen
gill. Cold jelly mess of a
boy shucked wide open. In-
vertibrate. Raw. There is a
whole sky at night in this
spoonful of shallot vinegar.
Little smarts of perpetual
annihilation drizzled onto
the open wound of me. I
never use his name. I feel it
hardening inside of me
like a symptom. O mother-
of-pearl, what at first
appears beautiful I clothe
in aragonite and conchiolin. A
mineral and glittering paint
brought forth from the very
centre, churning, of myself.

Still Life with Bananas

curved like dicks they sit – cosy in wicker – an orgy
of total yellowness – all plenty and arching – beyond
erect – a basketful of morning sex and sugar and sunlight

not enough things are yellow – only some flowers and
yolks and various melamine and plastic things – even
bananas are only yellow for a little while – they spend

most of their lives being green and brown – and who talks
about the green and brown – the underripe and overripe fruit –
that no one will ever display in a basket and no one will eat

you took all of my yellow days – every moment of bright
pleasure – clouded – coloured in – and now there is nothing
uncomplicatedly phallic – meanwhile the world goes on –

a chequered tablecloth is laid – there is a dining chair –
bentwood arms – will you ever draw it up – sit opposite –
apologise to me – mostly people don't know they've done

something wrong – mostly apologies are bullshit – and
what would yours sound like – how could you apologise
for unpeeling – for filling up on my life – for tasting

me – pressing your mouth to the flesh then leaving just this
mottled old rind – it's hard to look at bananas – it's
hard to be in the sunshine which is always making things

unreasonably golden and yellow and better looking
without asking for permission – fuck off sunshine – I
say on the hard days – like today – when not even this silly

fruit can distract me from my ridiculous sadness – just
once I want to see a banana that looks like a dick and
laugh – just once I want to see a dick and not think about you

Still Life with Pestle and Mortar, Copper Cauldron, Jug, Salt Dish, Onions and Cloth

What's being ground up in your little filigreed pestle and mortar? I can smell paprika or maybe lavender, as if someone were preparing for an exorcism.

And what's bubbling away in your bright copper cauldron? Some dark meat softening, perhaps, separating from the bone.

And what's inside your green jug? Green. Prismatic. Like how the mallard's head is green and prismatic. That fucking rapist. That shiny-feathered gang rapist.

When I cut onions, I weep. I am not the only one this happens to but it feels like a unique and singular sadness and then I start crying for real. Any excuse. And is there salt in your ceramic salt dish? Spread it onto my wounds, please, all of which lie beneath the skin.

In the Jardin du Luxembourg I watched a group of mallards surrounding one brown duck – holding her under the water with their orange and webbed feet, taking turns on her. And now I cannot pretend any more that I didn't know what was going on. And now you cannot pretend any more that you don't know what is going on with me. He groomed me and he touched me and I will not wrap this up in pretty words like how a gardener wraps his just dug-up onions in a white cloth that is the colour of a cloud. Or the colour of the delicate skin of my inside wrist. Or the colour of the delicate skin of my inside thigh. Or the colour of the delicate skin of my groin, penis, foreskin, scrotum.

His love was this kind of grinding. He put all the pieces of me into his pestle and mortar and he ground and he ground and now all that's left is this odd indescribable spice. This bitter sand. This molested pigment. Watch how I colour everything with my incredible brokenness.

Pestle. Mortar. Cauldron. Jug. Salt dish. Onions. Cloth. This is the very order of things. The vibrating symbols of my life. The subtext

and the sad truth which I cannot live any longer without spilling.
My lips open, jug-like, pour.

    The exorcism of poetry. The lyric reveal. The dark meat sliding off
the bone. The brown pigments smeared around and around until
shapes, the boy of me, emerges from the shadows. Do you see?
Do you hear? Do you believe me this time?

Still Life with Eggs, Copper Pot and Earthenware Pan

three white eggs
softly domed
in which I could
lay down my red
embryo and rest

when you are
born you are defenceless
not even an egg-
tooth to scrap and
hustle with and

this hereditary fear
of predators I
never got it 'how is it
there' the eggs the
copper pot

earthenware pan
with a weird cone'd
handle segmented like
an ionic column
pointing you out

and the mystery of hands
just out of frame
who put all this to-
gether and thought
yes that's it

and what was their
trauma was it little like
mine and what was
their trauma was it
big like mine

in the kitchen it is
harsh and noisy
copper glinting and
crashing someone has just
cut the head off a

rooster who is pump-
ing out blood a little
bleeding head is sing-
ing on the straw like
orpheus o my

wattled little demi-
god sing for me
your molestation aria
this is your big
moment bb and

you will not be silenced
but here in my
egg it is luminous
earth all white out like a
protestant cathedral

bleached vaulted
ceiling reaching up up up
everywhere the colour
of salt crystals the
clerestory a

sky where the
clouds are so very high
and you think o
wow even the sky
has turned white

today white
which is the colour of
understanding do you
understand yet
I was an egg

in someone else's
body once gleam-
ing prick of un-
harmed yolk I
am made of

equal parts
salt and song and
calcium carbonate
hexagonals and I will
survive this

Still Life with Carnations, Amaryllis, Peonies, Primroses, Irises, Pansies, Tulips, Butterflies, Marble Table and Pineapple

I chose this map of carnations, the thirty-seven sharp eyes of an ornamental pineapple.

You say you want me to talk about all of these things but I think the cherryade-red amaryllis, flopping down like a dog's tongue, is loud enough.

There is so much softness in the back of a leaf, like the pale reverse of a knee or the worn patches on your mum's coat – these suede and veined swatches.

True plenty is untranslatable.

Did you know he grew flowers from seed in his back garden and they were the models. Boy choir of stalks and buds.

My eye opens onto gesso-jewelled blooms that are impossibly from different seasons: the open-mouthed shouts of peonies, puce-hooped primroses, pink irises that are like the little churches you make with your fingers.

Do you know how to be happy like these flowers know how to be happy? My supernumerary harvest.

O the drama of a top-heavy bouquet which is something like your mum asking, what did you do to encourage him, lead him on. Which is breathing out the scent of anxious-preoccupied.

When you worship plenty, you also worship lack. The wall behind – raw plaster, negative space – anti-green gloaming and crepuscular.

Wind-up toy butterflies. Cut pansies, plastic-bright, scattered about the urn. You know what they say about boys who spend their boyhood in flowers.

Come, lay your forehead on the cool marble table. It is eighteen hundred and eight. The tribunal has yet to be assembled.

He spread chalk and rabbit-skin glue onto the canvas. A primer to make every calyx and corolla seem lit from within.

Imagine seeing a pineapple for the first time, the golden-lozenged shock of it, its sweet yellow blood. I can hardly remember anything which happened before all of this.

Craquelure blooms across the surface of these tulips, which are like little boy faces fracturing into variegated shards all the colours of we who have had no childhood.

Chimeric child of cytoplasm and cellulose, what did you do to encourage him, lead him on?

Still Life with Two Rabbits and Hunter's Satchel

Still so fluffed, so velvet that I want to press my cheek
to their tufted bodies – and would they be warm or cool,

these little quilted deaths? See I need this kind of comfort,
this arch softness, for I have been lonely a long time now

afraid of being touched, afraid of touching but I can touch
the dead, can't I? Run my fingers along their stilled bellies,

stroke their limp paw-pads, the odd little leather splotches,
place my fingertip into the satin envelope of each long

and ruminant ear, kiss each black and shining eye. Who
am I asking permission from? Who is even listening

to this interior and lineated monologue about the death
of the softest most beautiful things, that soil-scented space,

and the silence that follows the almost-human screaming?
From the sienna burrow of the canvas this silken pair,

this velveteen brace, these downy hindguts come scurrying
into their own deaths and have they died just for me

so that I might feel a little bit more alive tonight? This night
which is thick and violet and brush-marked and descends

upon the poet, that desperate little boy – quivering cottontail,
dunce – trying to figure his way forward by touch only.

Was I a kind of sacrifice? Given, allowed, consumed –
so that some other boys might be saved? Did my life mean

less? Did he get to keep one or two kills lying there – pliable,
soft entropy – on the marble shelf? A kind of altar to the many

and expressionless gods pacing up and down the gallery halls
only sometimes stopping to stare into the shimmering flanks

of these breathless offerings – deciding which to give life
and meaning to. Reader, I don't need to tell you what the

rabbits symbolise. I wanted to be the last little ruined boy
but no one will allow it. It is two thousand and twenty-four

and his victims are lining up like dead game spilling out
of the hunter's satchel and are innumerable. Forgive me.

Still Life with Apple, Ceramic Dish of Apples and a Pomegranate

I survived by being still.
Still as this red apple
on a wooden table top
and each time, afterwards,
after he had done what
he wanted with my body, I
packed all the little red
apples of myself – each one
slightly bruised, bumpy,
pock-marked, worm-scarred,
spored, mouldering – deep
down into the ceramic
dish of my body. Dissociative
I now know it's called and
didn't tell anyone who loved
me. Compartmentalisation
maybe. *A symptom is a word*
trapped inside the body
and I have so many words
trapped inside my body –
each one red and burnished
and hasn't aged at all.
Words. Like. Ruined. Fault.
Pricktease. Molestation. Shame.
Each one painted so perfectly
the colour of a hot coal
or a fresh graze. And I have
so many symptoms. Or the
colour of an apple smuggled into
Sainte-Pélagie prison in 1871

by your sister. Numbness. Or the
colour of an apple watching
from the wooden table top
of your teacher's desk. This stillness
is a kind of psychic wound. As
he arranges your body into a
still life. Apples. Ceramic dish. A
cracked-open pomegranate. These
repetitive and distressing images.
All the glistening and painful
reds beginning to move, to run.

Still Life with Fly, Iris, Finches' Nest, Moss and Poppy

A fly is crawling over everything. Even the fresh blue iris frilled like a salamander's neck. Even the finches' nest where the little speckled, borage-coloured eggs haven't opened yet. Even the botanically-accurate moss that looks soft like an old blue-green jumper. Even the Van Huysum blue poppy staring you straight in the eye like a school bully.

Absorption. Fly half in shadow, half of shadow. Little clockwork golem. Shit-eating angel. Such delicate filigreed wings. Just one, two strokes from the painter's smallest brush. Alive for a day now scratching his head over centuries of trauma. Blue fly. Blue whorl. Blue boy. I am losing track of what is going on around me. This baroque blur.

He is not a casual gendering. He is peritraumatic. A blue light through the iridescent cuticles of his wings splits into radiating foliage and flower-shaped shadows like how my mind fractures itself into that groomed boy, this sad adult. Did those bullies push you into his arms? Changes in one's sense of time are common symptoms during, after.

A still life is a kind of ghost. Everything painted is dead now. These are ghost flowers, spooky little fly. O I have feelings inside of feelings, such compound feelings, like why can't I just fucking die and be done with all this annihilation, and how I miss his petal'd conversation. Look down to find the fly on your own arm. You are in bloom.

Still Life with White Asparagus

Spear of slug-hued light, phallic of course, dirty tip.
Shard of gathering cumulonimbus askew on marble.

The inexpressible, these muddied shades, lives in me.
Washes of colour I can barely truss words to. And

language cannot help. The word 'anger', such a frail
conceit for the sallow-mauve tint that fizzes within.

It took me so long to ask for help – ecru or swan's
semiplume – that perhaps it is my fault after all. I

cannot decide. I judge myself as I judge these words.
Opaque. Nodules of smoky quartz and topsoil. Sapphire

undercoat humming with ruination. Are these feelings,
then? Asparagus and loamy glints. A dulled iridescence.

Evidence suggests the actual truth of it can hardly be
enunciated at all. I have things in me that are so dark

I cannot even write them down. That I might be *the Boy* [. . .]
by the Burying Ground staring into the asparagus-shaped

grave of who I might have been, unmolested, alights
from within the swirling mass of soiled and vegetal

colours over which this language, life, is a tiny pontoon.
And Manet's punctum of violet, extinct light pierces

shoot-like, spear-like – a perennial smart. I do not want
this single stout stem. I do not want this sfumato self.

Still Life with Rose Bush, Rain and Moths

I have been still life. Tenseless.
The Rose Leaf Miner perches. A
Large Yellow Underwing
shows no yellow. Don't say,

'I have made an arrangement
of my pain and it is shining'. Nor
how the beauty of antennae
or wing might alleviate this terror.

The varnished dark, resplendent
panel, that stretches on endless,
elastic and un-dying behind me. This
silvered rain, this spill of dew

which could be read as 'tears', or?
I grieve for my monstrous,
crenulated body. Its knotty
pausedness. Thorny song.

Still Life with Cornflower

That one little Prussian to mid-blue peep. Singular cornflower
among the whole cornucopia. Lapis rosette wrenching on me,

my lyric wound: just what he did to me, just what I let happen
but can a boy really be said to 'let anything happen'? Un-

answerable question at the taproot. So much crisp hurt in these
blue petals. And always the bloom's corolla as a schoolboy's face.

My face straining to understand how all this lives on in me
the way this solitary cornflower, hurt-sickle, lives on and on.

A curious kind of life being trapped under varnish, craquelure
forking above like these blue and livid occurrences flashing

into language. Like the bending of the boy's anther-like mind,
filament body – now entirely inseparable from flower. Blazer-blue

bud unfurling. O give him a little peace – wreath strung with
hyacinth, narcissi, that cornflower – he was, after all, 'a boy'.

Still Life with Cup, Irises, Pheasant and Cardoon

there
is
a
silenced
drama
here
a
juxta-
positioning
the
golden-
filigree
cup
of
irises
the
strung-
up
pheasant
its
red-
sash
throat
each
conferring
through
texture
petals
vs
feathers
rot

vs
blood
o
how
the
rendered
candle-
light
makes
each
quill
each
stalk
pop
how
easy
it
is
to
personify
them
they
are
two
men
looming
out
of
the
dusk
they
are
two
men

suspended
in
the
prism
of
this
glossy
moment
they
are
two
men
on
the
verge
of
a
painterly
darkness
only
one
of
the
men
is
a
boy
and
this
black
box
this
pin-
hole

camera
this
still
life
should
have
been
a
safe
space
but
some-
body
had
to
cut
and
some-
body
had
to
kill
and
some-
body
had
to
hang
and
some-
body
had
to
drain

all
the
blood
out
of
this
soft
bird
and
some-
body
did
some-
thing
much
much
worse
and
the
poet
is
here
blushed
cardoon
their
rooted
form
a
little
soil
scattered
about
them
they

have
been
digging
down
to
the
supposed
centre
of
things
and
what
they
find
they
will
make
beautiful
complicit
and
it
will
not
be
allowed
to
hurt
any-
one
any
more
ever
again
even

the
scaled
and
orange
feet
hanging
down
like
a
curse
they
will
make
them
into
a
charm
and
all
that
black
lacquer
they
are
polishing
it
up
like
onyx
like
agate
and
it
is

shining
even
the
irises
all
wound-
dark
and
livid
almost
rotten
almost
for
a
moment
look
like
they
might
be
un-
furling
just
a
little
bit
further
or
is
it
my
eyes
and
the

o
my
god
gold
jot
of
forgive-
ness
stippled
like
pollen
dead
centre
of
the
canvas
suddenly
clear
suddenly
re-
focusing
every-
thing

Still Life with Chrysanthemums

The chrysanthemums are open.
The chrysanthemums are golden.
The chrysanthemums are turning
their little molten ruffs to me,
their toothed inflorescences, their
bullion'd and mane'd throats and
saying with their perfume which is
their voice and saying with their
pollen which is also their voice:
you are safe and he will die soon,
you are safe and he will die soon,
you are safe and he will die soon.
Fold your mind into this aureate
softness. Any threat is ancient,
historic, decades past. An oracular,
motherly tincture. Fire-balm.

Still Life with Silver Cup, Copper Bowl, Spoon, Apples and Hazelnuts

for Daljit Nagra

Tangle of vertices – ovoid, hemi-sphere tilting, lolling –
like how there is a knot in my mind, intractable knot

of being groomed. *And sights that disgust you like half-
emptied glasses.* And a delicate queenliness of clinking,

curved shadow of seolfor, solid confection, on his tongue.
The life of the victim is still a creative one: glints, highlights,

I arm myself with these bright particles. Eye-yomp toward
orifices ringing, the wound of a bowl's yawn, stretched

lenticels of an apple's skin breathing and gold. His frontier
of brun cup shadows, pinked! *Still life will, above all, change*

into life in action. Cones reconstruct the cones. Hermetic
hazelnut birthed from suffocating wood to burnish. Copor!

By which I mean: vulnerability alights in me, uncluttered.
The lambent thatched earth. Linseed suspended, consolable.

Still Life with Grape

I enter the grape
push through pale
green flesh like a
fog and lay my
hurt these little
eggs at its core larval
white and sticky
eggs which will never
hatch but instead
become the source
of light O radiant
jade globe illuminated
beauty centuries
on the edge of rot and
spoil never have I
seen such greenness
pure shock of
opalescence every-
thing is tinted like
looking through a
stained glass martyr-
dom I will die
here be broken down
into my smallest
parts constellated
like the grape
but not just yet

Still Life with Plums, Melon, Peaches and Moss-covered Branches

And all those plums, a startling shade of thunder – like
look at the bloom on those plums! I never understood before
how you could call discolouration, this full body scar,
a bloom, blossom. And a melon in shadow like something
that hasn't been grasped yet like how maybe transference
sends me into the arms of these difficult men who will hurt me
and not let me heal. Maybe. How to be happy when happy
is not even a thing. I want to be like these three peaches
you haven't even noticed yet. Each one a yolky ginger dawn
coming up and tinting everything this crackled gold. O
to be peachy keen! I will be again. And it's not my fault
that he found me because I was moss-green, downy, singing
of life – like these branches, the last symbol, that snap me open
with a kind of just-been-carried-in-from-the-garden realism.
Still life yet still growing. So keep on growing, Richard.

II COY

after Andrew Marvell

Many people still don't know what grooming really is, beyond 'something people do to children'. They don't know what it looks like, so to speak.

GEMMA CAREY

. . . extort your reply
By finding any device to hack through
The thickening shades . . .

DENISE RILEY

. . . you deserve this state . . .

ANDREW MARVELL

i

I complain. I run years, refuse –
tear up, forehead flood and fire.
My heart worms, my skin dew,
every strife and slow devour of
him. Still, and thus, I complain.
At last this prey find sound – no,
song and roll back this years for you
to the grave's time of him and I.
Nor to praise but to try and be hear.
Nor to praise but to think yet lower
and through. Nor to praise yet to
stand, at last, in the gaze of all this.
Still and thus and now, I complain.

ii

A rough love him
and I. His gaze –
this bird of
prey with marble eyes –

find my quaint
virginity. Desarts
sun on skin.
My youthful hew

to ashes conversion. I
coy. A rough
love turn to
rough embrace. And.

iii

That which I cannot sound I may yet song.

I had be private, ecchoing in this preserv'd vault.

For years I had no sound but his sweetness, his lye.

Thus I go slow. I song last. Least. The lower.

That which I had nor sound I may still song.

iv

Our long love's no day but a soul
on fire. A bird in roll. Fine marble
dust in my eye. Flood of rough tear.
Humber-state. Ecchoing morning
pore into eternity. Last ashes and
lower. Ten-hundred-thousand worms.
A tear into a winged. Slow walk
into the grave. Vegetable turn vault.
An empire. A world lye. The time – no,
life – of iron. That which I deserve.

v

But coyness were a crime. My.
For him charriot to my gates and
praise, praise, praise! And such a

sweetness ecchoing may devour
the world and my. Were I coy?
May-be but rather quaint, youthful.

Coy be time's complain. And his.
Eyes down, skin fire and grow to
rubies state yet I were nor willing!

Still, for years I find my crime. My
part. My make. My quaint. My
coy. Him crime I cannot find.

vi

I should run, you state! Roll. Transpire, soul-like, to nor
show. Be dust in a vast desarts. Or bird. I should'st have,
I should. Yet I be slow and were by then all his – his
prey, his found pleasures, skin-ball for his sport. Now,
I would run. I do run. Each and every day. Back away
from his long breast slow hurrying into me, into me.

vii

My heart conversion to a rubies in the fire of him.

My breast to marble – a vault – which may make song.

And pass on, be winged and – *please!* – ecchoing into none.

And be none like how I had be none; and be none still.

This strife in my – I long for sound – I long for nor sound.

viii

His love tear my from the world,
gates my in iron. Lady, thou –

each and every and all go and
    I walk into his slow-chapt heart.

I life in his empire now; slow time
of marble. Day, a year and vaster still

pass into this private place which
be nor fine and yet be of embrace.

    And I be nor fine so I cannot nor be
with him; the slow and strife worms do

let the bird. Down eyes, down skin,
down breast. I deserve this. An devour.

ix

Vast rubies strife my breast. I forehead one, two
but ten, a hundred more and vaster still hurrying
into my skin and preserv'd. Each embrace, adore,
each lust-instant of him make a rubies. Him found
rubies in my skin and left his rubies there. This be
my skin complain, the pow'r of him which pass
lower and lower and into each and every pore and
ecchoing. This rough age preserv'd. My fire-state.
My rubies eternity. My rubies which do nor show
and yet be hear. My rubies which be the strength
and time of iron yet be nor a strength to my. My
rubies which be nor beauty and yet make beauty.

x

Let go of
him? I cannot
and thus I
make a fire
of my ashes. Let
go of him? I
cannot and thus
I grow from
tear to tide to
flood and
back. Let go
of him? I
cannot and
thus I let his

worms into
my forehead,
eyes, breast,
heart. Let
go of him?
I cannot and
thus I lower
myself morning,
each morning,
back to his
rough-hurrying
embrace. Let go
of him? I
cannot and thus
I make my life
this still life
preserv'd, part-
him, part-I.
Let go of
him? I cannot
and thus I
grow to devour
my state in
his place and
skin my each
and all with
this iron and
think-strife. Let
go of him? I
cannot and thus
I may find a
rough pleasure,
sweetness of
tear, in this

long complain.
Let go of him?
I cannot! My
eternity be
with him vault.

xi

I part long to be hear yet these near two-
hundred sound be nor my song. They be
of him. No, nor of *him* yet a years back him.
And back still a ten, a hundred, a thousand;
vast worlds of him and song. Thus song be
of all and thus be of none. This world of
sound before my life which now find my life.
I think rather I be found by this found song
and thus my song, song my and thus be
part-I and part-song; part-him and part-all.

xii

I had my time,
my tide

slows. The grave's
a fine and

place; I roll there
but be nor

private. Him
be there to.

Him be into
every state

of my life
thus my grave's

a vault for two.
I cannot be

virginity
for worms; this

lower state –
devour yet nor

to dust,
to lye there

in his marble
embrace

still and alwaies –
him last make.

Him had
my time. Him

had my
grave. Him

had. Him had.
Him had.

xiii

And yet the years back him do sport with song –
no lady, no crime – a pleasure in sound be all!

Thus do I make a strife with his song – conversion
him to bird of prey while him were honour-hew.

And thus do I sport like him. (No, I be coy. I lust
for his song. Devour his song. Make him lye).

All song be a sport. All sounds be prey. Bird
may devour worms. Yet worms may to devour bird –

bird winged, bird song – for him may complain
at my rough make. Him – *his sound* – refuse my.

Him do be of pow'r then! May-be him do be a
bird of prey – may-be I an devour by his song.

Yet I try to honour him. All. Still, a crime to find
crime with the years back him. And yet more

crime – *I languish* – to find a crime in all song. An
ecchoing of my rough life – *the ashes* – in each!

Lower than song be which? A long
to roll back years and nor refuse
but be nor with him at all. Nor
ever near him. No coy. No gaze.
No bird and no prey. None. Just still
and rest youthful. So transpires I,
my song, long for a cannot-be-
world. This my slow and tear strife. My
desarts. Lower than song be my
love for him. Him had honour once –
and we had a sweetness, hurrying
but once, and then this – *please!* – may-be
I still be prey! Him were alwaies
strife. To him, honour were a sport.
Lower than song be that *I* sport
with him. That I were coy, an am'rous
pleasure find, to be of his gaze,
in his gaze. Yet I be to to
youthful and in my heart – *think!* – I
refuse him alwaies. Lower than
song be that I be nor of honour
so I must nor sound nor song. Yet
a song cannot alwaies be of
honour, and to may lye; may-be
song alwaies be – *in sound!* – a sweetness
and lye. Lower than song be my
complain for all complain be but
of one! One part. One side. One strife.
One marble tear. Lower than song
be that I conversion all love
to worms within my languish state;

I cannot – *nor none!* – be of love
now. My vast and vaster crime. And
lower than this, that I deserve this.

xv

Time pass and yet be still in my heart.
Do I had a heart? No, rather this rubies –
still charriot of slow, slow time. And alwaies
more time. I rest in youthful all this
years – yet my fine skin do age. And him,
no, him would nor be am'rous to my
now which be of pleasures to my –
to be nor gaze on, to be none found.
Which day may him find the grave?
Which day may him, his pow'r, grave?

xvi

To sound a song with no hew – for my world had no hew.

Sun, rubies, tide, skin pass to ashes; all be ashes-hew.

And lower into me – *if eyes may find!* – this marble- no, still ashes-hew.

I life this way. I be nor make for hew. I deserve this nor hew.

And yet lower, lower I do hear a pore of – *this instant!* – hew.

All songs charriot a hew, sounds, with-in. A worm – *a him!* – of hew.

If my song be of hew then may-be I may had – *at last!* – some hew?

Mistress to languish and yet – *please!* – let my deserve this now hew!

xvii

A coy life to turn his thirty-thousand make
into fire, ashes, dust, desarts which all still be
nor enough. And yet in this turn – *at last a turn!* –
I *do* make. Conversion all this found in the
vault of my to song. Turn his fire to an am'rous
fire in my forehead! And be of instant fires now!
And be hurrying back to him – *in think!* – to
find more would for this sound-fire, that this may
grow! O(f), the lust-sound as my fire-song
devour him! May-be I place coy, this coyness,
into the fire to, for to think of him now be to
think of my. My languish. My life. This all be
my. Years refuse yet now I embrace this part.

xviii

If my breast be a vault, then I gate him in –
him be the worm in my. Yet this worm do
sound and his sound ecchoing make my song
to sweetness. I do nor adore him yet charriot
his sound with-in. And song now for more
life. Yonder life. Vast and vaster! Years back
all hear him yet now you may hear my –
found, a part of and yet – vegetable sound!

xix

I had turn his song
to languish yet
now his song
turn my up – a
rough tear through
my rough life
to make a sun:
    him be there in my
think, my song, but
not there, there.
I forehead his strife.
I prey on my one.
I be the worm in my,
now. Yet if I
think this then
    I may to refuse this.
Grow! And this
think be the sun
of my morning and
dew. At last I find
a pow'r hear:
    I run to the sun.
I devour the
sun. O(n) I be all of
the sun! If I had
life in the desarts-
eternity of him
which may I be
but a sun?

xx

For at my lower, lower place, I may still song
a song of praise. For at my lower, lower place,

I may still make. If a complain may grave, be
this the grave of my complain, (n)or the run-on? Coy,

a coyness, do nor make my deserve all this. And
thus, a slow sweetness do sit with-in: though to-day

be of worms – *O(n) grave beauty!* – I will to-day
love. And this cannot be a crime. For him show me

how to prey so now I prey on this day, this instant,
in song. For I had no crime. None. Now nor then.

xxi

And if the sun will nor stand still. And
if a bird will alwaies prey. And if the fire
will to make ashes. And if rubies be alwaies
in skin. And if a tear will alwaies to flood.
Then which for I, now. And which for *him*.
No, which for I. I be willing, at last, to
sound my soul – show and be transpires!
This prey still be prey yet make. And hear.
And think of him and nor of him. And be
of pleasures. And praise. And run on and on
till state be winged. And tear through the
iron gates of him to find an I. And life in this
day. And life in song. And pass, ecchoing.

III   THAT BROKE INTO SHINING CRYSTALS

22 Crystals after Arthur Rimbaud and Wyatt Mason

*Unearth the crystal, hold it in your right hand again and ask,
'What was it like down there? Was it comfortable, please say.
Was it fearful, please say.'*

*Take notes, take MANY NOTES. The crystal will translate
the way to the poem(s) with you.*

C A CONRAD

. . . et les pierreries regardèrent . . .

ARTHUR RIMBAUD

Citrine

From within the mine – shale, spinel crusts and pyrite shards that glitter blackly and I can see the vein of citrine open itself like a molten wound, candescent, in the mountainside.

O such citrine opulence winking away in the pumiced curvature of the shaft, shimmering in the clefts, alighting the aperture crags – honeyed eruptions, golden fists of grown-stone, flaming roses and urine prismatics!

Like the eyes of some beautiful faggot this citrine seems to glisten with tears and pulls every shattered boy out of the earth. And such a painful harvest, volcanic, opening the throat chakra and mouths canary-bright with the runic jumble of revelation.

O citrine – patron stone of the molested, sunny eliminator – crown us with your polychromatic glittering and awe-flecks. Offer abundance to those of us quarried. A boy is igneous.

Red Jasper

Thirty-eight and I am learning a lot about rocks – this stone nurtures, this stone guides, this stone clears, this stone detoxifies.

Red jasper – routinely water-worn, etched, red-shock when split – carries past words, images within its brecciated fissures. Blooded elixir. Is boy-like.

All my life I have been meeting others who suffered the same pressure – sub-atomic, neurological – of a love which is not love at all but instead is this attrition. Red sand.

You shouldn't even think about all that any more says so many people and websites. So I get busy writing poems. Conduits. Shamanic journeys into the sub-mantle realm. It turns out that I am raw, powerful.

I feel my purpose crystallise within me. Scabs – little platelets of red jasper are crusping up, forming over my entire body. Something important is happening to me.

Obsidian

I am the seer – obsidian-eyed – envisioning men, etched and crystalline, holding hands to the horizon.

I am the savant, nose-deep in polished texts – *provides a grounding chord! Blocks psychic attack!* Rain bejewels the library window.

I am the hitchhiker pacing the obsidian road. O sing to me a healing song and vibrational. Sunset is a veil and refraction deep within the rock – a molten and glowing internal fracture.

I am the toddler in a cave whose only god is this twinkling stone – burnished sheen on black giving me a little light – limitless.

All paths lead then. When it was the end of the world I was still expected to get up in the morning and go to school. The air smells burnt – solidification. O the tragedy of the crystallographer who sees every path but cannot choose another.

Kyanite

Bury me in kyanite, a blue translucence, I want to read the earth. Beetle scratchings, hag stones, calligraphy of root systems all flash past. Here I am learning the buried tongue, the mineral subtext of things.

Sewers drain into me – filter, amplify – till I am eye-to-eye with space-blue rock, fossilised screaming. Things are becoming abusive – petrifying.

At these depths, I am a comet and he is the moon – astonishing and submerged. I gravitate to within his thrall – this orbit, a molestation and deep inside my blue cells I am buried and scratching alive. The elongated smallsword. The dense particle, rewritten.

These bitter, untranslatable hours and even my body has become a wand of kyanite – absence of light yet somehow glittering – cerulean and pearlised skeleton, a dusting of fractures like icing sugar.

And then you, my illumination – cyan-lux urtext – feeding me these uncut words; such mantle knowledge. O I am blue in the lips – your plutonic mouthpiece!

Peridot

O for a few more of those pre-trauma days, when life was as dazzling as a piece of raw peridot and all my hours were grass stains and beach glass and sycamore leaves glinting and shifting and irises spears shooting up, up, up!

And lime cordial, molten peridot, thick and gloopy as time in the bottom of a glass – sliding, coating. And a fresh bruise when a bruise was just a bruise and could fade. And the gloaming when even the gloaming was green – pear-green and freckled sky, mustachioed wisps.

But he is here too – fission-green flaw deep within the facet – giving off his own glow, blinding, disorientating. A crystal kind of man, polymorph, because he still has something to teach me and I don't know if I will ever truly learn it.

Protective stone, keeper-away of evil spirits, where were you when I needed you? His touch was mantle-hot and ruinous; intrusive, extrusive.

I am always looking for a new frequency – hoping to recover some peridot shard of myself in this lapidary of broken things – but I can only translate what is already here and not transform. Hats off to the crystallographer who is watching chartreuse ions precipitate into livid rocks, I am toxic – petrified ectoplasm – luminously bonded to my past.

Carnelian

Between the scrubland and forest – living orange and lotus –
a carnelian-lipped lad is meditating, bringing all this into being.

His third eye – vibrational, humming – is a raw-form carnelian.
Even his apricot body, lifeforce, seems hewn out of carnelian.
Bronze light edges across the treetops – sharpening, clarifying.
An ornamental koi has swallowed the sun.

This carnelian of him – peerless, precious enough for a diadem or
the cover of some illuminated manuscript – stores the knowledge, a
hardened-by-earth drive, of all us faceted, hammered into and glints.

Dearest heart, cut out and shining, but you cannot be broken –
even by this sheer terribleness.

Dearest body, where is my body? I am entombed in this carnelian
mind; bevelled and tumbled synapses, peachy-pink shrieks.

Dearest mind, is ennui a singular type of PTSD?

The listless jeweller spots a flaw in the carnelian and gets polishing,
smoothing down the filigree igneous bubbling of overripe orange
and glittering stone-flesh. Artificer knuckle-deep in pyroclastic
shards.

The world seems amber-tinted. Rusty throb.

Lapis Lazuli

for Hannah Lowe

Stone – that is like the sea, that is like the sky, a blue scarf
tied around a boy's head, his eyes rolling upwards in pain or in
knowledge, a blue feather on a boy's wing – I am swallowing you
down.

I remember the churning flow of the river through the spired
city, glassy ropes and spray. My hands blue in the running water and
reaching for something. My breasts, the bumpy and bluish areola
around each nipple. The crinkled skin around my eyes shot through
with blue lace. A bruise, five-fingered and lapis-dark.

Every one of me was just as damaged. My mind – pitch-navy
geode – has become a fane, fossilised, to suffering. I don't know what
it is to live without this opaque fracture, strike and dip. I am negative
bias. I am nothing. I could never have avoided this life.

But there is gold in this blue darkness. Lapis disbands martyrdom.
The golden veins spell out what happened. Amplifier, confront!

Lapis time is deep time. Blue time. Constellated rock and cimaruta.
Eye of Horus excavating his seismic assaults, the buried silences.

O these shining avenues – these churches turned to temples in
the lapis-light of my translation. A new architecture, saxe and auric,
assembles!

Red Tourmaline

C'est moi! The dead boy buried deep as a seam of red tourmaline –
shamanic stone on each eyelid, tongue scrying through the earth and
seismic.

We are in the south. Scarlet leaves buffet the school. We follow the
red-brick road to reach the empty classroom. Spatial echoes of those
moments, his touch, are a kind of consciousness. The jam-coloured
hexagonal pillars vibrate.

Bricks rewind to sand. Sand rewinds to strata. Strata rewinds to
igneous and magma and every fault is birthing raw tourmalines –
the molten-rose heart of the world.

And singing, they rock back and forth – the tourmalines are
like eggs and another *he* is hatching. Fabulous pussyfooted beast,
embryonic seer, already taking you deep into yourself and
diminishing fear. A natural radiation, his tears are devas.
Transmigration.

Don't tell me assault was *transformative*. Don't tell me *when the
worst happens and you just move on*. Don't tell me anything but
tourmaline and repair – rock: quantum and shimmering, crimson
then clouded rosettes.

O ancient striations and ruddy-blush fractures – incarnation of
my long body – a shared molestation is the key to these crystals;
deepening the stain from pink to red.

Fluorite

I can't see straight anymore. I'm lost and in crisis mode, some dumb boy-bird flip-flapping at the cornice – iridescent my wings and tinged with fluorite.

Or I am a bear with fluorite-tinted fur and bleeding gums. My eyes to crystals wide staring into the old traumas. Overstimulated, starving and drag.

Or I am a donkey, braying grief and hunger, shrieking into the long grass that is all the moving greens of light through fluorite, the rainbow keeper.

O matrix of igneous rock! O solid aquarium spilling out little glints of violet! O pre-trauma morning-brain before you remember what happened! Last year you were in the city and each window dazzled like a healing layout and you cried on every man – Roman and marble-handed – who passed.

Or I am a boy, little glinting thing, who was groomed. Polished-up, faceted, girdled – a glittering kind of ruin.

Blue John fluorite – tricolour, personality disorder of a rock – carries the spirit of change. The happiest year of my life is yet to come – revising old poems and writing new ones and stopping only sometimes to think *lui!*

Rhodochrosite

In the woods there is a crystalline bird whose cry is like a baby's.

And there is a sundial – shadow stuck at some point in the p.m.

And there is a ground nest sheltering little pink, translucent and lightly furred animals. All their mouths are open and you can see right down their scarlet throats.

And there is a church swallowed up by the pinkish sand where they have to lower you down by rope to pray.

And there is a lake whose surface is tumbled then polished then tumbled – pink stones shuffle and wet below the surface.

And a teacher's car – red warning to pink faded – swallowed up by a thicket. The windows that held your silence now hold a pink sky. Sore empyrean.

And there is a cherry tree weeping little skin-pink flowers.

And there is a raw rhodochrosite crystal inside your pocket, against your skin – heating up to body temperature. Vibrating. Dissipating. O banded rhodochrosite of the solar plexus – gem *par excellence* for mending the molested.

And there is an emptiness inside of you – the dream of childhood always ends with ennui – that bleeds into this translation. The closing of the third eye, grey-pink gland.

And you do not have a home apart from these words so you keep on walking, reciting.

In the woods there is a crystalline bird whose cry is like a baby's – were you ever that young? You blush a rhodochrosite-pink.

Onyx

Out of the lyric rises this mineral being! Raw onyx body, banded, blackest marble-effect. Jet fault lines, inky wounds glitter within his mesmerizing whole. He has survived the mantle's forge.

All the dark colours of my life – bruise, scab, lesion, intrusion – dance, seem to radiate from him. Trauma-shard. Holder-onto of previous injuries. He is a kind of asymptomatic mirror – activated, in crystal grid, tetrahedron, layout.

O ashen-eyed onyx boy, your chiselled arms are canons erupting – you are stabbing me with bright black shadow. Bright black like how the insides of my eyelids can be bright and black and quavering; these molten pixels of anti-light.

I have placed all of my hurt into the lyric space of him – crypto-crystalline landscape vibrating – and wait, shining, for a new vitalism. Vast end to dis-ease.

Pink Opal

Can crystallography cure? Can these grown stones temper triggers? Forgive my boyish questions but I am still a little pink in the head.

O matrix, cherry and fire – seductive rock and clarifying, reorienting my mind – these wounds are new eyes. The rained-on city transmutes to papier-mâché canyons and pink-dwarf dusk and rosy crystalline refractions – my amygdala Venus!

I live within these luminous fissures and gorge. Even my flashbacks – his face, his hands that broke me – now break into shining crystals. Are opal-tinted, seraphic.

Opal shard, slight as a fingernail and skin-pink too, activates clairvoyance. Is anti-shame. I am not broken but deformed, reformed. I am taking responsibility. The startlement of all-over salmon interior colours and ripe coral fragments of a whole to find a new and abstract whole. Quadrant 001 – repaired, unrepairable.

O I have been one era-long resistance stage – petrified tongue fleck and always asking the wrong questions. Now, homonuclear – dazzle!

Celestite

Blue-point and celestite sky. Bizarre cartography of bridges – some oblique, some falling. The illuminated bend of the canal beneath, charged with cerulean light. The domes and towers clustering together like hyacinth spears. The bridges strung with masts and poles seeming to glitter like orthorhombic celestite wands in the watery luminescence – finite, infinite.

A melody pierces! Criss-crossing the structures and frames, ebbing, sousing. Seemingly alien then catching a minor fifth and leaping up into an aria. A little changeling boy, angelic even, his mouth opens onto cloud colours: translucent, spheric, cosmic.

He did not stop singing. He is singing now. Dodecahedron notated and transmuting. Disc of spinning cyan energy. His five throats unblocked and ego-less. His revelations, celestite-sharp and eddying the brilliant water with cadenced runes.

This fractal, truthful, coloratura alloys the shining grey-blue fragments – blue-point and celestite sky, bizarre cartography of bridges – of himself, covalent-like and coalescing, into one blued I, but always creating unquiet, opera buffa, within the cavities of all this.

Amethyst

Here they come! Lorries dense with lilac lads – Marys posing in purple spandex – puce puppies and piss-slaves and pierced twinks – amethyst-wigged drag queens serving face, body – daddies painted in mulberry leathers! A hundred floats sparkling and catching the light like split-open geode clusters, glitter and feathers raining down.

And coffins, crystalline and shining, raised high on chiselled shoulders – and jam-velvet canopies sewn with semi-precious stones twinkling like the starry skies of your village childhood – and painted placards and lavender badges and pink triangles, vibrational. O amethyst, stone of transmutation – centring and violet-bright – all this energy becomes love, soothing and self-soothing. Our veins are tinged purple!

And mares, massive and iris-skinned, their legs and flanks stretching down from the amethyst empyrean. Our feathered caps are stroking their furred and calming bellies, low-ceiling and periwinkle safety.

No one of us are damaged. No burning, molten attrition, mantle's pressure here – just this effervescence, the continuation of light, retina and optic nerve disco. Amethyst is living iron and single point scrying – prismatic absolute protector!

Even our ruts, pure amethyst-fire and burnished, as we round the bend –

Lapidary

Petalite, rose rocks strung around his forehead. Beneath, his semi-precious eye-spheres – fire opals flecked – swivel and dart.

His cheeks are cinnabar. Calcite molars shine out of his mouth – are moon rocks.

His chest is a split-open watermelon tourmaline geode – wet-look and twinkling. And there, a raw rose quartz quavering away for a heart.

I made this man – crystalline golem – from all the broken and cut shards in this lapidary. Who would do as I say. Who would never hurt me. Who understands that fuckery is a kind of elixir – sex, a salve.

My own prismatic son of Pan – two-spirit tiger's eye molten in your balls and leaking. Orange sapphire for a dick, erect and glinting. I yawn open my sacral chakra, ache for your sheer rock-hardiness!

My lapidary bb, your thigh bones – bright and tumbled topaz – strut towards me. I am horny. I am shattered.

Selenite

Alchemical sea of
selenite and crystalline
upsurges. Moon-drawn
bridges, barnacles
shattering, spirals and
sheets stirring easterly
towards the white
satin spars of the pier –
nearly translucent –
which jut out into this
vision. O rare pre-
trauma memory! Your
gangplanks and girders,
piles and shafts, catch
the light – opening this boy's
crown and higher crown –
unfathomable link to the
light body and secret: this
inner-most shard of him
is un-touched. Ethereal,
angelic – Na_2SeO_3, the pre-
acid bond. And a fish-
tail selenite diving back
down into pressure and such
pure wetness. O he is
scrying for something
soul-like in this Jurassic
sea which just glitters
on the surface – free
radicals and tabular,
phantom, amorphous –
and, in splintering, drowns –

Magnesite

I am counting isotopes. I am counting isotopes, coccoliths,
igneous intrusions, prismatic bonds, physical weathering, faults.
I am counting and the sky is falling. It has been falling my whole
life. Magnesite vibrations fill the house, bubbling up, bringing to
the surface all forms of self-deceit.

A horse, magnesite-white, is walking across the earth, through
every field, orchard, back garden. His legs – attachment, separation –
move as if they love being alive. Momentarily, he looks a bit like
a unicorn from an old tapestry, clinquant and stitched into being.
O to be able to see a unicorn!

Somewhere in the world a histrionic lad is translating all his
trauma into poems. Every day he feels as if he is eating broken glass
so checks and rechecks his food. His brain is nobly – porous to
suggestions, obsessions – a raw-form magnesite; un-tumbled, lobal,
fluorescent grey like the sun has just slid behind a cloud and it's
October.

Let us all return to our ologies: translation and bringing the
hemispheres into harmony. Let us all resume the exhausting work
of pretending to feel better. Let us all smile into the magnesite sun,
irisless eye, like we mean it. Our thoughts have a kind of physics –
the mind is quantum – and these rocks are sparking up!

And that horse, queer animal, breaks into shining crystals! My
existence is the stringing together of these temporary and geopathic
reliefs. When the raw-form magnesite made an elixir of water,
I gobbled down the chalky gem essence. Desperate and sighing;
back into the broken, fractured, body. Mine.

No more lying to yourself. Magnesite is astral bright, illumination,
such radical acceptance.

Emerald

for Emily Berry

On the hillside little boys are twirling and looping and catching the light and falling down into the grass which is the colour of raw emeralds, shifting and bright.

The field is a body. Wild grass rippling over breasts and muscles, the jut of a hipbone. Some of the grass is trampled down into mud like a battlefield – screams catch the air. Some of the grass is spread over little hillocks like shallow graves. Some of the grass is cut into a bit, desire lines and goat paths, leading to all the places you ever dreamed of going but didn't.

Emerald grass at your feet and an emerald seam in the sky constellated by flickers, green pictures. The light is innocent, primitive. Its green ray aids – unearthing, X-raying.

The little boys are tearing up fistfuls of emerald grass and throwing it into the air and dancing in the green and prismatic rain. The little boys themselves seem green and made of emerald – more fairy than boy. Crystalline, detoxifying – these ones are shining.

All the greens are very close to your face right now. The landscape holds you like a basket. Overcome. There is no abyss just this immense patience. Recovery is possible.

Rose Rock

for Daljit Nagra

When the world is chipped away to a single rose rock – *radial and rosette sprays*, tongue-coloured thing – I will find you, angelic consciousness, the boy genie who was raped.

Translation is a kind of telepathy – link to the light body – and you my genie, crystalline and circumlocutive, both inhibitor and release. How did you escape the Ithyphallic battlements? Their soupy and burning jets?

My genie is trans-dimensional now – trauma-dark and four astonished eyes – and his petalled words, this rock rose, are the bridge. A beach for two boys where words run over their bodies like crystalline water and the sand is birthing these hard roses.

O rose rock – elemental trauma-flower, genie's insoluble whisper – only your voice can distract me from this hyperarousal and slipped inside me like how water precipitates into porous and sandstone layers. I am permeable. You, ethereal.

Dress up, dance, pick the sand from off your tongue, form a protective grid around the house, write a poem which opens a French window onto a slight vein of hematite gifts a beige-pink tint to the roses.

The sand erupts like anger – rose rock, rock rose – a new vibration on the earth. Opaque truths forced into imagery and carrying the imprint.

Jade

Jade is present tense and opening my finely-muscled structures – these pulses purify. Jade's destination is the future of who will touch my body with love. A green and mineral thumb – detoxifying – jade *is* love.

Working, balancing between my hips – an instrument, wand – to keep me from harm. Piercing my mind too, soapy green dream-stone, absorbing my terror that he will not withdraw. And such a deep green like laughter ringing out in the forest of my body. The velvet of a prince riding out. A turtle's chin and old beak. A lime spot on the sun's disk.

I open my cavities to workshop him in flesh and these old bodies – houses, traumas, the infection of molestation – fall away. Silicate tranquillity descends on a cellular level.

O jade, your diaphanous song inside and mint-greening me – my cerebrospinal fluid, my parasympathetic nervous system flush fern. My castle, ruination, is besieged with glittering and dappled sage. O jade, I slip you further inside and it is not winter.

The loop is broken. A viridescent ribbon sighs to the floor. My triggers, signalling molecules, unwind. Jade is moss-soft palms and consensual. Jade is superhuman raw and beautiful machine verdant. Jade is the multiverse written into variegated stone and banded – there I am and there I am and there I am happy!

Bloodstone

for Owen Willetts

Blood on a stone changes that stone into a bloodstone. Hybrid rock of igneous hurt. Alligator-quartz spotted through with iron oxide intrusions. The trauma of attrition, inclusion – dangerous, livid – now polished up and raw-cut shining.

Every time you are touched you change a little, are molten. Currents, geological phenomena are playing within you like ostinatos. You are several parts civil war – smashings and reformation. Children look at you and think you're a grown-up because you are tall but it's not as simple as all that.

It's as simple as SiO_2.

It's as simple as this wound I hold open for you – catches the light, a glittering of blood-spots and geode-blooms. The chaos of trauma precedes transformation.

O bloodstone, my audible oracle – sing to me your sheer song of chemistry and intuition-sharpening. Most blood-rich courage giver, you have bled too. Fragments – ruddy inclusions – included in a host rock are older than the host rock itself and what am I to make of this?

Martyrs' stone. Heliotrope. Hematite. More crystal than man these days.

Quartz

I kissed time. The unspeakable hour. Quivering and fractured pale.

Everything was broken and dark. The tumbled-down palaces. The shattered water. The bodies of soldiers heaped in the clearings. But I was walking and the semi-precious stones opened their eyes and looked on.

I heard the language of minerals – a kind of glinting tinnitus – spelling out elements, properties. Helical gyre. Kirlian Camera. Aura.

White light flared and spread up the silver birches, living wands, and his body – shining cluster, spirit-cleanser – was cast in quartz.

One by one, I lifted his veils in a dance and I was dancing. I chased him into the city where he painted the steeples and domes and pub signs into bright shards. I was running – an amethyst-head – drunk on light.

I caught him. I swallowed him – pure elixir, natural computer – down. I woke up.

I mean really woke up. And it was my day – pure crystalline attention – my bones biomagnetic, reclothed.

Notes

I

'Still Life with Rose' refers to Margareta Haverman's painting *A Vase of Flowers*, 1716, and Rachel Ruysch's painting *Tulips, honeysuckle, apple blossom, poppies and other flowers in a glass vase, with a butterfly, on a marble ledge*, c.1691–1694.

'Still Life with Lobster, Fruit and Timepiece' refers to Abraham van Beijeren's painting *Still Life with Lobster and Fruit*, 1650.

'Still Life with Lemons in a Wicker Basket' refers to Juan de Zurbarán's painting *Still Life with Lemons in a Wicker Basket*, c.1643–1649.

'Still Life with Basket of Songbirds' refers to Clara Peeters' painting *Still Life with a Peregrine Falcon and its Prey*, c.1612–1621. It also uses words from Colnaghi Gallery's exhibition notes to *Forbidden Fruit: Female Still Life* and from *Translucent Matter* by Alicia Vogl Saenz, both indicated by italics.

'Still Life with Three Roses' refers to Jan Van Huysum's painting *Glass Vase with Flowers, with a Poppy and a Finch Nest*, 1720, and Margareta Haverman's painting *A Vase of Flowers*, 1716.

'Still Life with Snail, Oyster, Spoon and Shallot Vinegar' refers to *Still Life of Oysters and a Prawn on a Ledge with a Snail and a Butterfly*, attributed to N. Adama (active late 17th century), and Jan Davidsz. de Heem's painting *Still Life*, 1664–1665, which also features a snail and oysters.

'Still Life with Bananas' refers to Pierre Bonnard's painting *Basket of Bananas*, 1926.

'Still Life with Pestle and Mortar, Copper Cauldron, Jug, Salt Dish, Onions and Cloth' refers to Jean Baptiste Siméon Chardin's painting *Still Life with Pestle and Mortar, Pitcher and Copper Cauldron*, c.1728–1732.

'Still Life with Eggs, Copper Pot and Earthenware Pan' refers to Jean Baptiste Siméon Chardin's painting *Still Life with Kitchen Utensils, Cauldron, Frying Pan and Eggs*, 1733. The poem is also in grateful dialogue with various ideas from John Berger's Peter Fuller Memorial Lecture, 'The Infinity of Desire', given at Tate Modern in 2000, from which it also utilises a phrase, indicated by speech marks.

'Still Life with Carnations, Amaryllis, Peonies, Primroses, Irises, Pansies, Tulips, Butterflies, Marble Table and Pineapple' refers to Jan Frans van Dael's painting *Still Life with Flowers in an Agate Vase Placed on a Marble Console*, 1823.

'Still Life with Two Rabbits and Hunter's Satchel' refers to Jean Baptiste Siméon Chardin's painting *Still Life with Two Rabbits*, c.1750–1755.

'Still Life with Apple, Ceramic Dish of Apples and a Pomegranate' refers to Gustave Courbet's paintings *Still Life with Apples and a Pomegranate*, *Three Red Apples*, *Still Life* and *Still Life with Apples and a Pear*, all painted between 1871 and 1872, as well as a visit he was paid by his sister Zoé when she smuggled fresh fruit and flowers into Sainte-Pélagie prison in Paris where he had been imprisoned for his involvement in the Paris Commune. The poem also uses an idea from Jacques Lacan's talk 'Joyce the Symptom', as told to me by Emily Berry, indicated by italics.

'Still Life with Fly, Iris, Finches' Nest, Moss and Poppy' refers to Jan Van Huysum's painting *Glass Vase with Flowers, with a Poppy and a Finch Nest*, 1720.

'Still Life with White Asparagus' refers to Édouard Manet's painting *A Sprig of Asparagus*, 1880. The poem also excerpts this phrase from Emily Dickinson's letter to Thomas Wentworth Higginson on 25 April 1862: '*I had a terror – since September – I could tell to none – and so I sing, as the Boy does by the Burying Ground – because I am afraid –*', indicated by italics.

'Still Life with Rose Bush, Rain and Moths' refers to William Gouw Ferguson's painting *Six Butterflies and a Moth on a Rose Branch*, 1690.

'*Still Life with Cornflower*' refers to Philips de Marlier's painting *Still Life with a Basket of Flowers on a Ledge*, 1634.

'Still Life with Cup, Irises, Pheasant and Cardoon' refers to Felipe Ramírez's painting *Still Life with Cardoon, Francolin, Grapes and Irises*, 1628. The poem is also in grateful dialogue with various ideas from John Berger's Peter Fuller Memorial Lecture, 'The Infinity of Desire', given at Tate Modern in 2000.

'Still Life with Chrysanthemums' refers to Henri Fantin-Latour's painting *Yellow Chrysanthemums*, 1879.

'Still Life with Silver Cup, Copper Bowl, Spoon, Apples and Hazelnuts' refers to Jean Baptiste Siméon Chardin's painting *The Silver Cup*, 1768. The poem also uses two phrases from Marcel Proust's article 'Chardin and Rembrandt', indicated by italics. The poem also recalls some loving advice given to me by Daljit Nagra, '*The life of the victim is still a creative one*', also indicated by italics. The poem also utilises several Anglo-Saxon words: 'seolfor', 'brun' and 'copor', which might be translated as 'silver', 'brown' and 'copper'.

'Still Life with Grape' gratefully speaks back to, and is inspired by, two incredible Mary Ruefle poems – 'Poem Written Before I was Born' and 'The Last Supper'. It also refers to Margareta Haverman's painting *A Vase of Flowers*, 1716, and Luca Forte's painting *Still Life with Grapes and Other Fruits*, c.1630.

'Still Life with Plums, Melon, Peaches and Moss-covered Branches' refers to Pierre Dupuis' painting *Prunes, Peaches and a Melon on a Marble Table Top*, 1650, and Louise Moillon's paintings *Cup of Cherries and Melon*, 1633, and *Still Life with Basket of Plums*, 1629.

II

'Coy' is a found poem, a vocabularyclept, which uses and playfully rearranges the words of Andrew Marvell's extraordinary poem 'To His Coy Mistress' as first printed in his *Miscellaneous Poems*, 1681.

Thank you to Helen Gardner, for her suggested modified spellings printed in *The Metaphysical Poets* (Penguin, 1957), which I am utilising. Thank you also to the British Library for their exceptionally helpful online and open access facsimile first edition of Andrew Marvell's poetry.

Thank you principally, and with apologies to, Andrew Marvell.

III

The twenty-two poems in 'That Broke into Shining Crystals' all speak back to Arthur Rimbaud's *Illuminations* but through the prism of various crystals and semi-precious stones – and their geological and healing properties.

In writing these poems I am indebted to Arthur Rimbaud for allowing me, unknowingly, to work with his crystalline language and queer, proto-Surreal and Symbolist landscapes. I am also utterly grateful to his translators – principally Wyatt Mason for his radical, lively and extremely helpful translations which shaped my experience of *Illuminations* – but also to Martin Sorrell and John Ashbery. And thank you also to Edmund White, Enid Starkie and Seth Whidden for their rich and inspiring biographies of Arthur Rimbaud.

I am hugely indebted to Judy Hall's extraordinary writings on crystals contained within her book *The Crystal Bible*, which I quote from in 'Obsidian', indicated by italics; and also to crystalage.com, tinyrituals.co, energymuse.com, thecrystalcouncil.com, sciencedirect.com and wikipedia.org for their collective and inspiring wisdoms. 'Rose Rock' is in grateful dialogue with various ideas from the Oklahoma Geological Survey, from which it also utilises a phrase, indicated by italics.

The phrase 'that broke into shining crystals' is a line from Arthur Rimbaud's poem 'Première Soirée'. The translator is unknown, but the words are used here with the kind permission of Kevin Watt and allpoetry.com where the translation appears. Thank you to the anonymous and talented translator of this line for giving me a focus, and title, for my sequence and indeed book. And thank you again, of course, to Arthur Rimbaud.

*   *   *

The book's epigraphs are taken from Emily Dickinson's poem 'The first Day's Night had come –' (410); and Peter Gizzi's poem 'Archeophonics', in *Archeophonics* (Wesleyan University Press, 2016), reproduced with kind permission from the poet. The quotes on p. 1 are taken from *The Last Supper* by Rachel Cusk, copyright © 2009 by Rachel Cusk, reprinted with permission from Faber & Faber Ltd and Farrar, Straus and Giroux (all rights reserved); and from 'Ode on a Grecian Urn' by John Keats. The quotes on p. 41 are taken from a *Guardian* article by Gemma Carey entitled 'I'm a survivor of child sexual grooming. It took me 20 years to know it wasn't my fault', reproduced with kind permission from the author; from Denise Riley's poem 'A Part Song', in *Say Something Back* (Picador, 2016), reproduced with kind permission from the poet; and from Andrew Marvell's poem 'To His Coy Mistress'. The quotes on p. 57 are taken from CAConrad's (Soma)tic Poetry Ritual #71: 'Grave a Hole as Dream a Hole' (somaticpoetryexercises.blogspot.com), reproduced with kind permission from the poet; and from Arthur Rimbaud's poem 'Aube'.

Acknowledgements

Thank you to the editors of the following publications in which some of these poems first appeared: *Poetry Review, Rialto, Magma, Perverse, 14 Magazine, Poem-A-Day* (Academy of American Poets), *Fourteen Poems, Catflap, Oxford Poetry, Under Your Pillow* (Victorina Press, 2023) and *Queer Life, Queer Love* (Muswell Press, 2021).

Profound thanks to Lavinia Greenlaw, Lavinia Singer, Jane Feaver, Hazel Thompson, Hamish Ironside and everyone at Faber. Thank you also to Matthew Hollis.

Absolute gratitude to my agent Emma Paterson.

Inestimable thanks to Daljit Nagra for his continued belief in my poems, support, friendship and close reading. Vast and joyful thanks to Edward Doegar, Hannah Lowe and Jane Yeh for their friendship, generosity and wisdom; also for reading and workshopping these poems with me. And beloved thanks to Emily Berry, who brought me three white roses and began a conversation which resulted in this book, and to Owen Willetts – 'courage giver'.

Additional thanks are due to Joey Connolly and everyone at the Faber Academy, including Keir Batchelor and Sarra Said-Wardell; ECW at Goldsmiths College, including Maura Dooley and Tom Lee; the Poetry Library; the Poetry Society; the Royal Society of Literature; the National Gallery; the Rialto and Michael Mackmin; Southwark Libraries; the Michael Marks Charitable Trust; the Arvon Foundation; the Jerwood Charitable Foundation and Southwark Park Galleries.

I am also incredibly grateful to the Society of Authors for a works-in-progress grant which enabled and supported the writing of this book.

Loving thanks to my friends for their kindness, support and continual inspiration: Tom Butler, Alice Dixon, James Anthony, Richard Crawley, Rebecca Perry, Amy Key, Alex Macdonald, Crispin Best, Celia Barlow, Simon Allen, Elspeth Henderson, Luke Roberts, Maurice Riordan, Rachel Long, Wayne Holloway-Smith, Jim Slade, Lærke Feld Andersen, Sam Taylor-Fox, Mimi Khalvati, Anna Selby, Oscar Kjell, Will Harris, Rebecca Morrison, Sophie Stanton, Talisa Garcia, Lina and Alex Mahdavi, and my godson, Isaac Dixon – the boy who 'is able to see a unicorn'!

Big love to my family – Gerard, Hilary, Linda and Rod Scott.

And so, so much love to my partner Daniel.